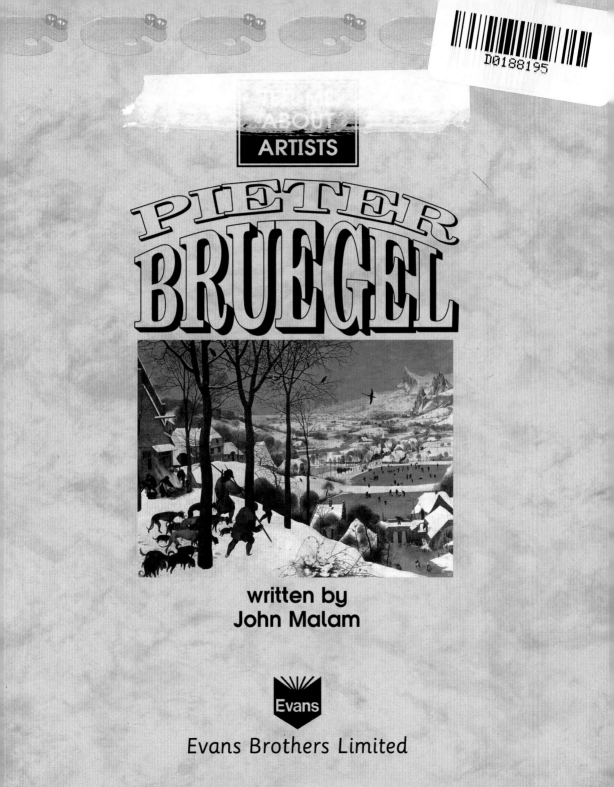

TELL ME ABOUT ARTISTS

PIETER BRUEGEL

written by
John Malam

Evans

Evans Brothers Limited

Published by Evans Brothers Limited
2A Portman Mansions
Chiltern Street
London W1M 1LE

First published 1998

Printed by Graficas Reunidas SA, Spain

British Library Cataloguing in Publication data.

Malam, John
  Pieter Bruegel. - (Tell me about artists)
  1. Bruegel, Pieter - Juvenile literature 2.Painters -
  Belgium - Biography - Juvenile literature 3.Painting,
  Flemish - Juvenile literature
  I.Title
  759.9'493

ISBN 0237518066

Pieter Bruegel was an artist. He lived 450 years ago, but no one can be certain when he was born, or even what he looked like. He painted pictures of ordinary people working in the fields, or playing games, or dancing. No other artist had painted quite like this before, and Bruegel became famous. This is his story.

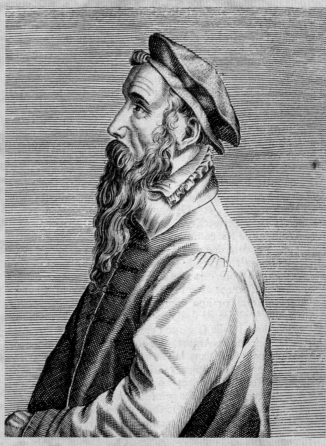

This drawing of Bruegel was made three years after he died. No one knows if it shows how he really looked. The artist drew it from memory.

Pieter Bruegel was born in a part of Europe called North Brabant. Today, this area belongs to Holland.

He might have been born in the town of Breda, near the North Sea coast, but we cannot be sure. The year of his birth is also a mystery. It could have been 1528, 1529 or 1530.

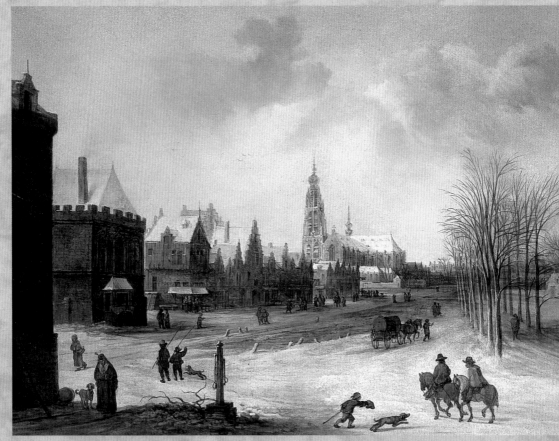

Breda, as it looked in Bruegel's time

Nothing is known about Bruegel's childhood. No one has found out who his parents were, or whether he had any brothers or sisters.

Perhaps one day an old document, such as a letter, will be found which will help to solve some of these mysteries.

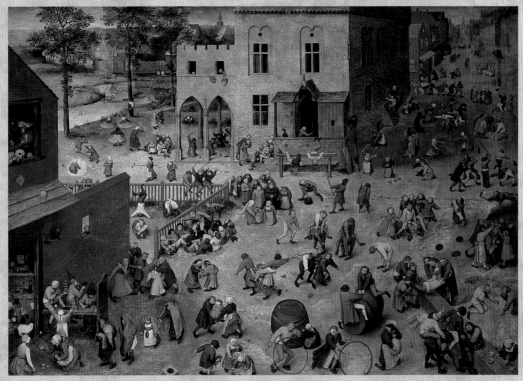

This painting by Bruegel is called 'Children's Games'. It shows about eighty different games played by children, such as leapfrog, walking on stilts, and rolling hoops. Bruegel probably played games like these when he was a child.

We do know that when Bruegel was in his twenties he left Breda. He went to live in Antwerp, a big city about 40 kilometres away.

In Antwerp he went to work for Pieter Coecke. He was a well-known artist who owned a busy workshop. Many apprentices, or students, worked there. It was where they trained to become artists. Bruegel became one of Pieter Coecke's apprentices.

An artist's busy workshop in Bruegel's time

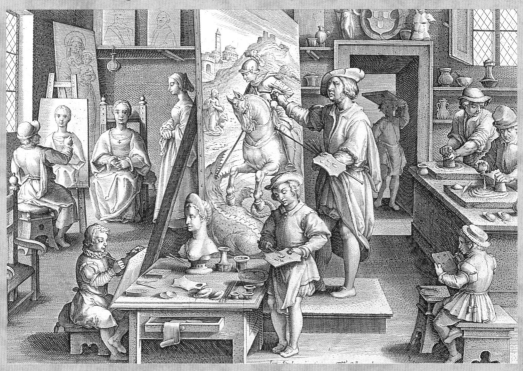

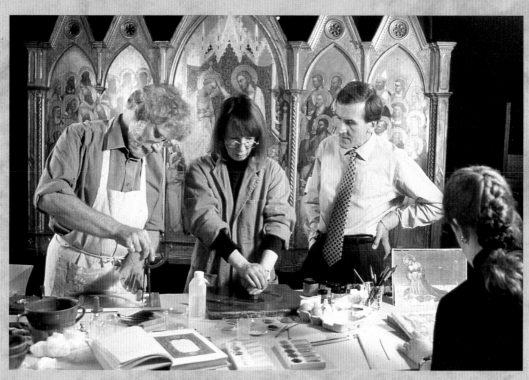

A picture from a television programme about how artists in Bruegel's time worked. The woman in the centre is making blue oil paint.

In Bruegel's time most paintings were made on flat pieces of wood, called panels.

Bruegel learned how to cover a panel with coats of chalk mixed with animal glue. When the surface of the panel was completely smooth and white all over it was ready for him to start painting on. He painted in oil paints.

By 1551, Bruegel had finished his training. In that year he became a member of the Antwerp Guild of Painters. This was like a club, which only fully trained artists could join.

Soon after joining the Guild, Bruegel went on a long journey to France and Italy. He was away from home for about two years.

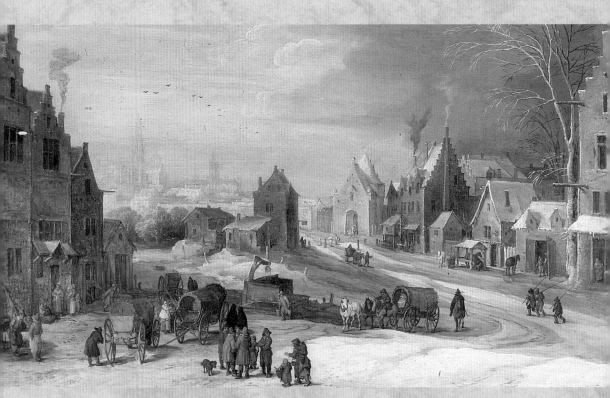

Antwerp as it looked in Bruegel's time, in winter

In Italy, Bruegel visited artists' workshops and studied paintings. He wanted to find out new ways to make his own pictures.

But it seems that what really interested him was the scenery he saw on his travels. On his way back to Antwerp he crossed over the Alps, a range of high mountains. He liked them and he began to make pictures of mountain landscapes.

The Alps are the highest mountains in Europe.

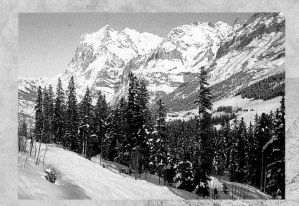

A mountain landscape, drawn by Bruegel after crossing the Alps.

Back in Antwerp, Bruegel worked for his friend Hieronymus Cock. He was a print-maker. Bruegel made drawings, and Hieronymus Cock printed them on to paper. He could make many prints of the same drawing. They were sold to the public.

This print is called 'The Big Fish Eat the Little Fish'. In the picture, Bruegel compares people with fish. It is about how big fish (greedy people) swallow up little fish (people who are not greedy).

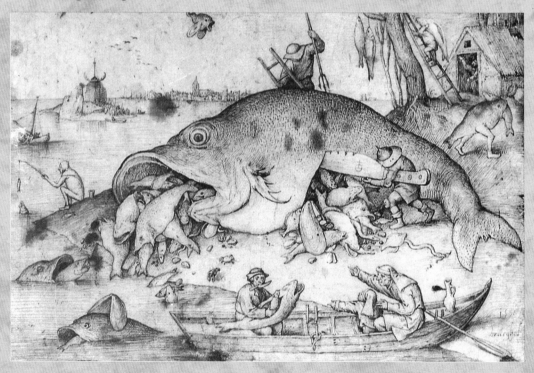

In 1563, Bruegel married Mayken Coecke. She was the daughter of Pieter Coecke, Bruegel's teacher. They left Antwerp, and went to live in Brussels.

Bruegel and Mayken had two sons. They named the eldest Pieter, after his father. The youngest was called Jan. Both sons became artists. Pieter made pictures of hobgoblins and fires. Because of this his nickname is 'Hell Bruegel'. Jan painted pictures in bright colours of flowers and landscapes. His nickname is 'Velvet Bruegel'.

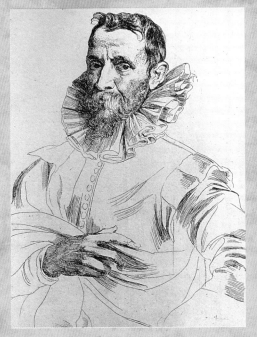

Bruegel's son, Jan

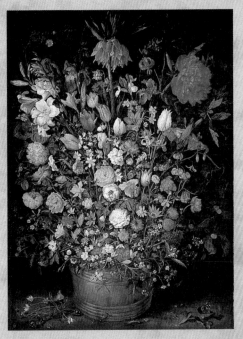

A flower painting by Jan

Bruegel painted his most famous pictures during the last few years of his life.

In a painting called 'Mad Meg', he painted an old woman walking through a strange land full of monsters and bad people. The old woman is carrying bags full of gold and silver.

'Mad Meg'. This painting was meant to make people think about how they lived their lives. If they were greedy, then perhaps they would end up living a terrible life in a dreadful place, just like Mad Meg.

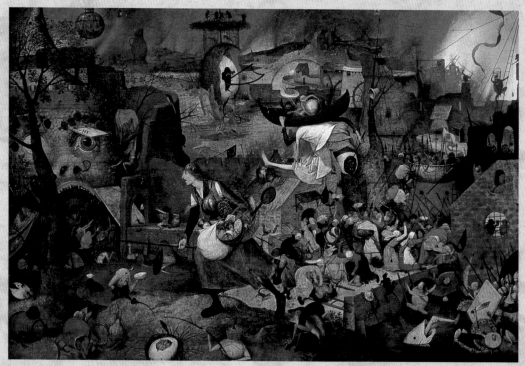

Paintings based on Bible stories were always popular with artists. In his painting called 'The Tower of Babel', Bruegel showed the tower described in 'Genesis', the first book of the Bible.

Bruegel made the tower look like a famous Roman building called the Colosseum. He had seen this when he visited Italy.

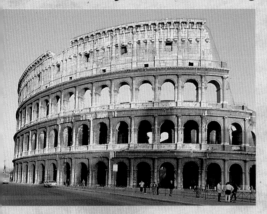

▲The Colosseum, in Rome

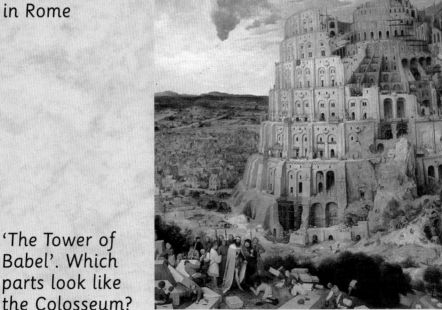

'The Tower of Babel'. Which parts look like the Colosseum?

Bruegel's paintings are full of detail. In 'The Hunters in the Snow', a group of hunters are returning to their village in winter. One hunter is carrying the fox they have caught. In the distance people are skating on frozen ponds. Some are playing ice hockey, while others are spinning tops. There are even firemen putting out a chimney fire.

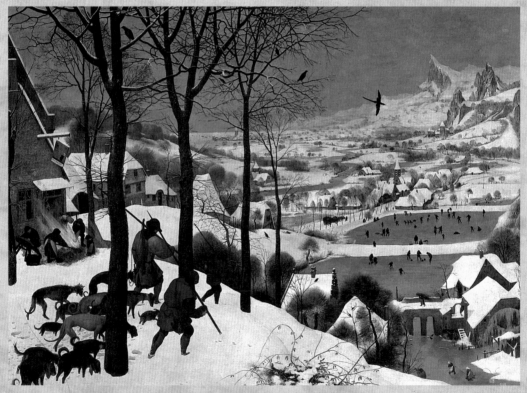

'The Hunters in the Snow' represents the month of January. Other paintings by Bruegel represent different months.

Another painting that shows a winter scene is 'The Census at Bethlehem'. In this picture, Bruegel made Bethlehem look like a village in Holland, and not like the Bethlehem of the Bible.

Mary and Joseph are at the bottom of the picture. They are arriving by donkey at an inn. A crowd of people wait to be counted as part of the census.

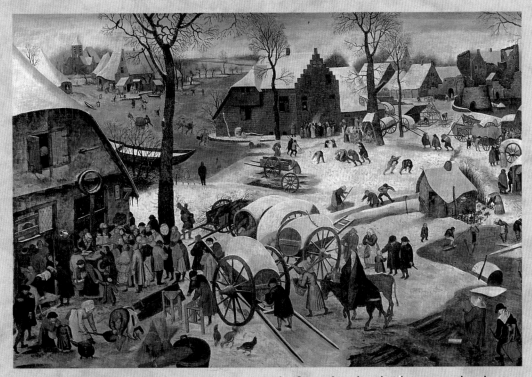

'The Census at Bethlehem'. Look for the little hut with the cross on its roof. Bruegel might have meant this to be the stable where Jesus was born, after the census.

Bruegel earned the nickname 'Peasant Bruegel', because he liked to paint pictures of the ordinary people he knew in Holland. In 'The Wedding Dance' he painted about 125 people dancing and talking in a forest clearing, after a wedding.

'The Wedding Dance'. Look for the bride. She is in the middle of the picture, wearing a garland in her long red hair. She is dancing with an older man, who may be her father. Some people now say this picture is not by Bruegel.

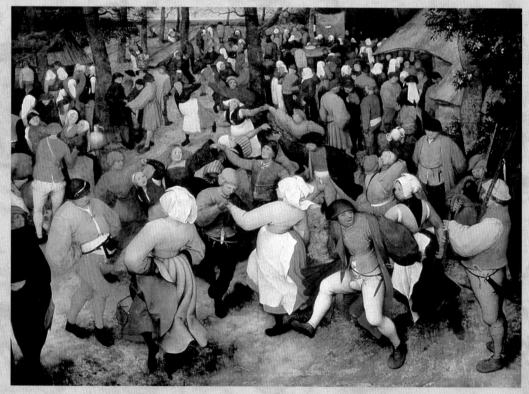

In another wedding picture, called 'The Wedding Banquet', guests are enjoying a feast of wine and pancakes.

The bride sits with her back to a cloth on the wall. But which man is her new husband? Perhaps it is the man passing the pancakes from the serving board. Or perhaps it is the man leaning back from the table, calling out for more wine to fill his empty jug.

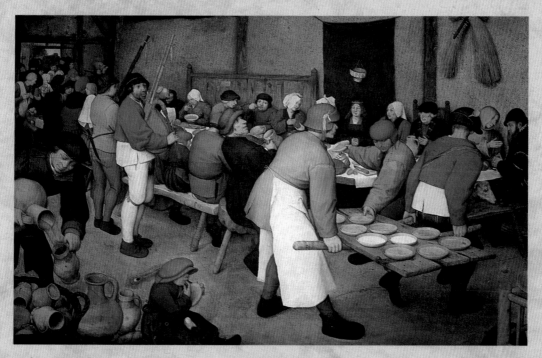

'The Wedding Banquet'. The serving board is actually a door. You can see its metal hinge.

Pieter Bruegel the Elder died in 1569, aged about forty. Many years after his death, Carel van Mander wrote about him in a book. He said:

"Bruegel was a very quiet and thoughtful man, not fond of talking, but ready with jokes when in the company of others. He liked to frighten people, even his own pupils, with all kinds of spooks and uncanny noises."

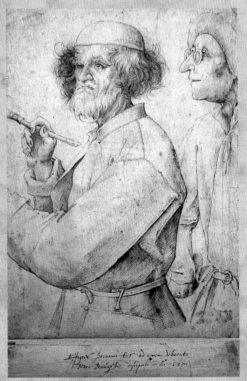

This drawing by Bruegel might be a self-portrait. He might have had long hair and a beard, and he probably did wear clothes like these.

Important dates

In this list of dates, the letter "c" before a date means "circa". This is the Latin word for "about". For example, "c.1528" means "about 1528".

c.1528–30	Pieter Bruegel the Elder was born, probably in Breda, a town in present-day Holland
c.1545–50	He learned about painting from Pieter Coecke
1551	He became a member of the Guild of Painters in the city of Antwerp, a city in present-day Belgium
1552–53	He travelled in France and Italy
1554	He visited Switzerland, where he made drawings of the Alps
1555–63	He lived in Antwerp, painting and drawing
1560	He painted 'Children's Games'
1562	He painted 'Mad Meg'
1563	He married Mayken, the daughter of Pieter Coecke, his teacher. They moved to Brussels
1563	He painted 'The Tower of Babel'
1564	His son Pieter was born
1565	He painted 'The Hunters in the Snow'
1566	He painted 'The Census at Bethlehem'
1566	He painted 'The Wedding Dance'
1567/8	He painted 'The Wedding Banquet'
1568	His son Jan was born
1569	Pieter Bruegel the Elder died, in Brussels
1578	Mayken Bruegel died

Keywords

apprentice
someone who works for, and is taught by, a teacher

artist
someone who makes drawings and pictures

landscape
a painting or drawing of the countryside

oil paint
a type of sticky paint, made by mixing a colour with oil from a plant

panel
a flat piece of wood on which a painting was made

print
a copy of a picture on paper

Index